Contents

Does everything grow?

No. Living things grow, but non-living things do not grow.

Humans and other animals are living things. We all grow.

Humans and Other Animals

wing

David and Penny Glover

FRANKLIN WATTS
LONDON•SYDNEY

First published in 2004 by
Franklin Watts
96 Leonard Street
London
EC2A 4XD

Franklin Watts Australia
45-51 Huntley Street
Alexandria
NSW 2015

Series Editor: Sally Luck
Art Director: Jonathan Hair
Design: Matthew Lilly

ISBN 0 7496 5545 3

All photographs taken by Ray Moller unless otherwise credited.

Kelvin Aitkin/Still Pictures: 17b; Mike Bluestone/SPL: 12; Fred Breummer/Still Pictures: 9b; Laurie Campbell/NHPA: 18b; John Cancalosi/Still Pictures: 25; . Martyn Colbeck/OSF: front cover r, 15t; Jeff Collett/Ecoscene: 9t; Roger de la Harpe/Still Pictures: 13b; Martin Harvey/NHPA: 23l; M & C Denis-Huot/Still Pictures: 21l; Mitsuaki Iwago/FLPA: 13tl; Klein/Hubert/Still Pictures: 13tr; David Lucas (www.dclvisions.com): 8t, 16. Joe McDonald/Bruce Coleman: 21r; W Meinderts/FLPA: 11t; Photogenes: 7t; Fritz Polking/Ecoscene: 17t; RobinRedfern/Ecoscene: 23r; Steve Robinson/NHPA: 18t; Jurgen & Christine Sohns/FLPA: 11b; Barrie Watts: 15bc, 15br, 25tl, 25tc, 25tr, 29b.

Every attempt has been made to clear copyright. Should there be any inadvertent omission, please apply to the publisher for rectification.

A CIP catalogue record for this book is available from the British Library.

Printed in Hong Kong / China

Plants are living things, too. Trees, flowers and grass all grow.

Non-living things do not grow. Bottles, bricks and bicycles are non-living things. They always stay the same size.

Cut pictures of living and non-living things from magazines. Make two sets - things that grow and things that do not grow.

Do all animals grow?

Yes. All animals grow.

New babies grow quickly. They need new clothes every few weeks.

Find some of your old baby clothes. Compare them to the clothes you wear now. How much have you grown?

As a crab grows, its shell gets too tight. The shell splits and the crab steps out of it. This is called moulting. A new, bigger shell then grows around the crab's body.

A polar bear has a thick fur coat around its body. A polar bear's coat always fits because it grows with the bear.

Do all animals have babies?

Yes. All animals have babies.

Every baby has two parents - a mother and a father. When babies grow into adults, they may meet partners and together have babies of their own.

A baby cow is called a calf. A calf is born after a cow has mated with a bull. The cow is the baby's mother. The bull is its father.

A baby duck is called a duckling. Ducklings have two parents. The mother is called a duck and the father is called a drake.

A calf is a baby cow. A duckling is a baby duck. Do you know the names of any more animal babies?

Where do babies grow?

Some babies grow inside their mothers. Others grow inside eggs.

A human baby grows inside his or her mother for nine months. Then he or she is born.

Humans and cows belong to a group of animals called mammals. Find out the names of other mammals. How do mammals feed their babies?

At first, a baby kangaroo grows inside its mother. When it is no bigger than your little finger, it is born. The tiny baby crawls through its mother's fur into her pouch, where it grows into a joey (a young kangaroo).

A crocodile lays eggs in a nest. Her babies grow inside the eggs. After two months the eggs hatch. The babies use a special tooth on their nose to break through the shell.

Do all babies look like their parents?

No. Some babies look like their parents, but others look very different.

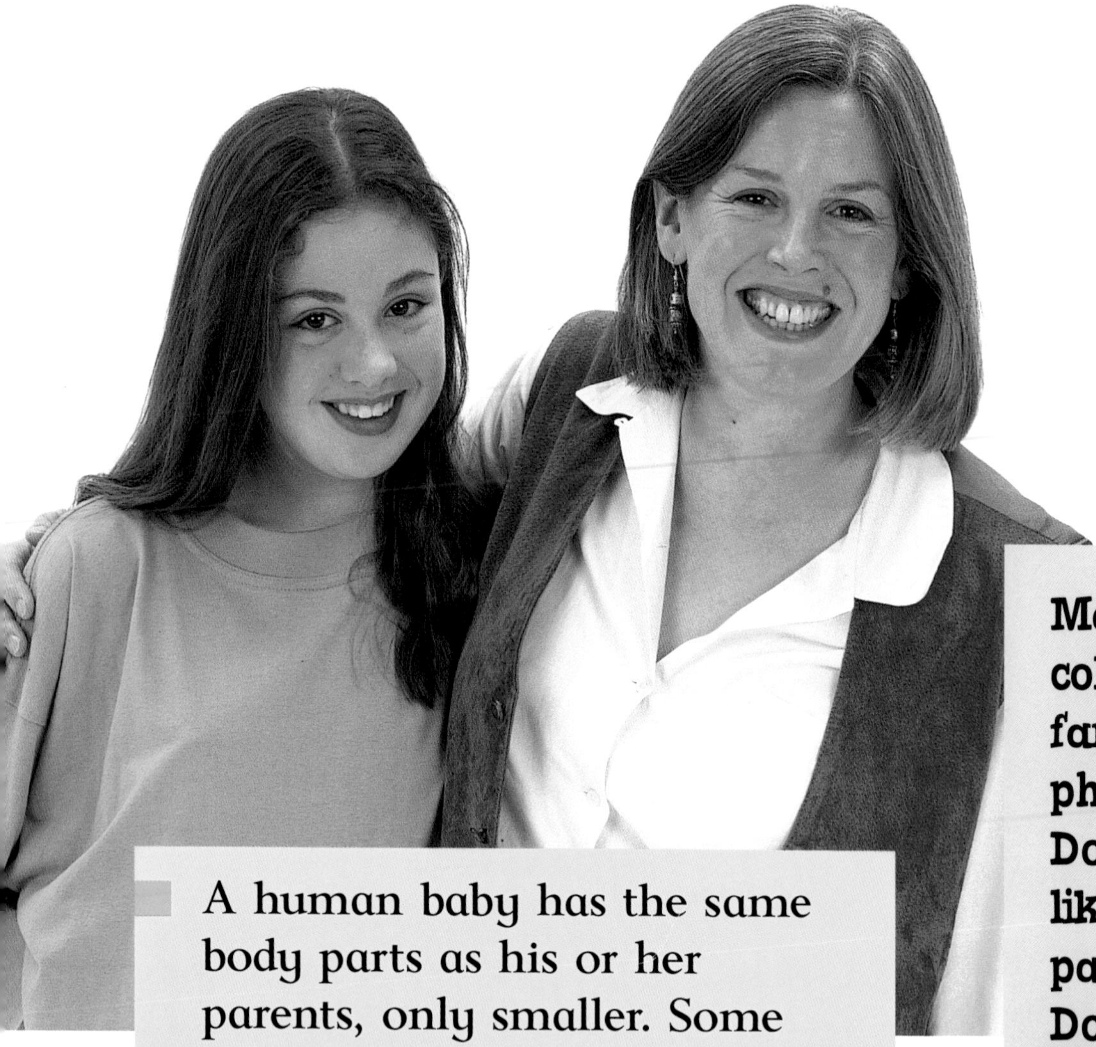

A human baby has the same body parts as his or her parents, only smaller. Some babies have faces just like their mother or father. But some babies look quite different!

Make a collection of family photographs. Do you look like your parents? Do you look like your brothers and sisters?

Like a human baby, a baby elephant is a small copy of its parents. It gets bigger as it grows, but it does not change very much.

A tadpole is a baby frog, but it looks nothing like its parents. It swims with a long tail and has no legs. As the tadpole grows, its legs grow and the tail disappears.

Who cares for babies as they grow?

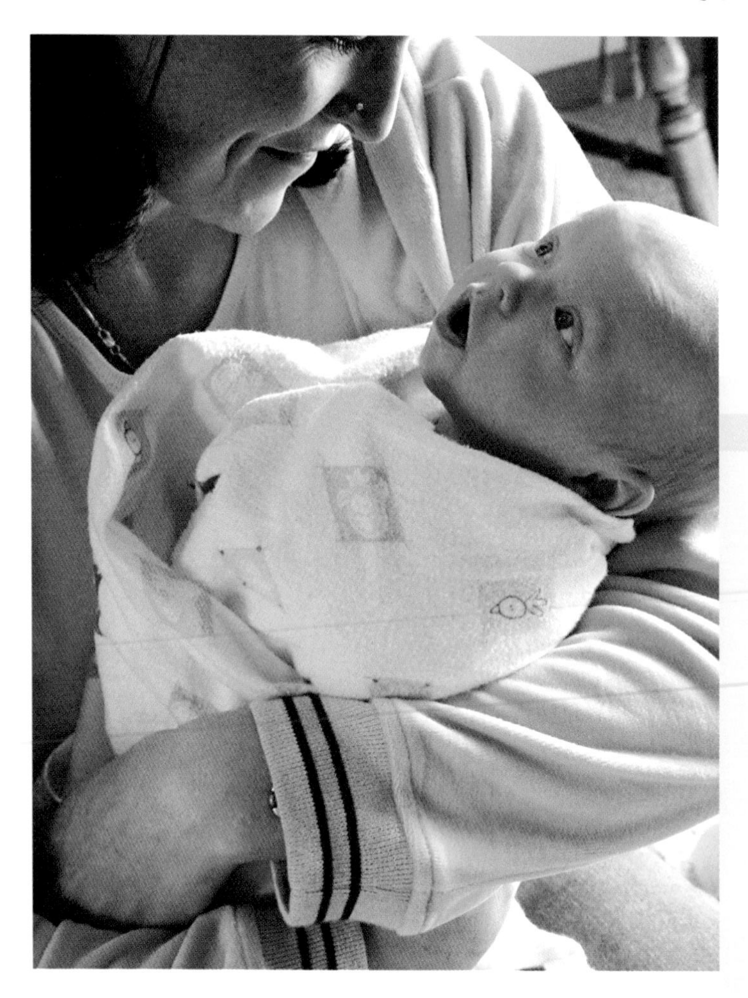

Adults care for babies as they grow.

A human baby cannot look after herself. The baby's parents care for her and give her love. If the parents cannot look after the baby, other adults will. The baby's brothers and sisters can help, too.

Pretend you have a baby animal to care for. Think of the different things it needs. Act out the things you should do to care for your baby.

Emperor penguins look after their babies well. The mother lays an egg and then goes to the sea to catch fish. The father keeps the egg warm. After two months the mother returns to feed and care for the new chick.

No one looks after a baby turtle when it hatches. It must find its own way to the sea and look after itself.

How do we learn as we grow?

As we grow
we learn new things by
copying, playing, listening,
talking and reading.

A baby is born knowing some things, like how to breathe and cry. But she cannot do other things, like sit-up and walk around. A baby's parents help her learn how to walk. Then she practises on her own.

Can you tie your shoelaces? How did you learn? Teach someone else how to tie a shoelace.

A young chimpanzee learns to fish for termites by poking a stick into their nest. It copies an older chimp who knows the trick. Termites make a tasty meal!

No one teaches a spider how to spin a web. It is born with this knowledge in its brain.

How tall do we grow?

Babies are all about the same height. But some children are small and some are tall.

All the children in a class at school are about the same age. But they are not all the same height. Different people grow at different speeds.

Mark your height on a wall with chalk. Mark the heights of other members of your family. Who is the tallest person? How much taller than you are they?

A baby giraffe is as tall as a man. An adult giraffe is as tall as three men standing on each other's shoulders. Giraffes are the tallest animals in the world!

A snake does not grow tall, but it does grow long. Some snakes grow up to 10 metres long.

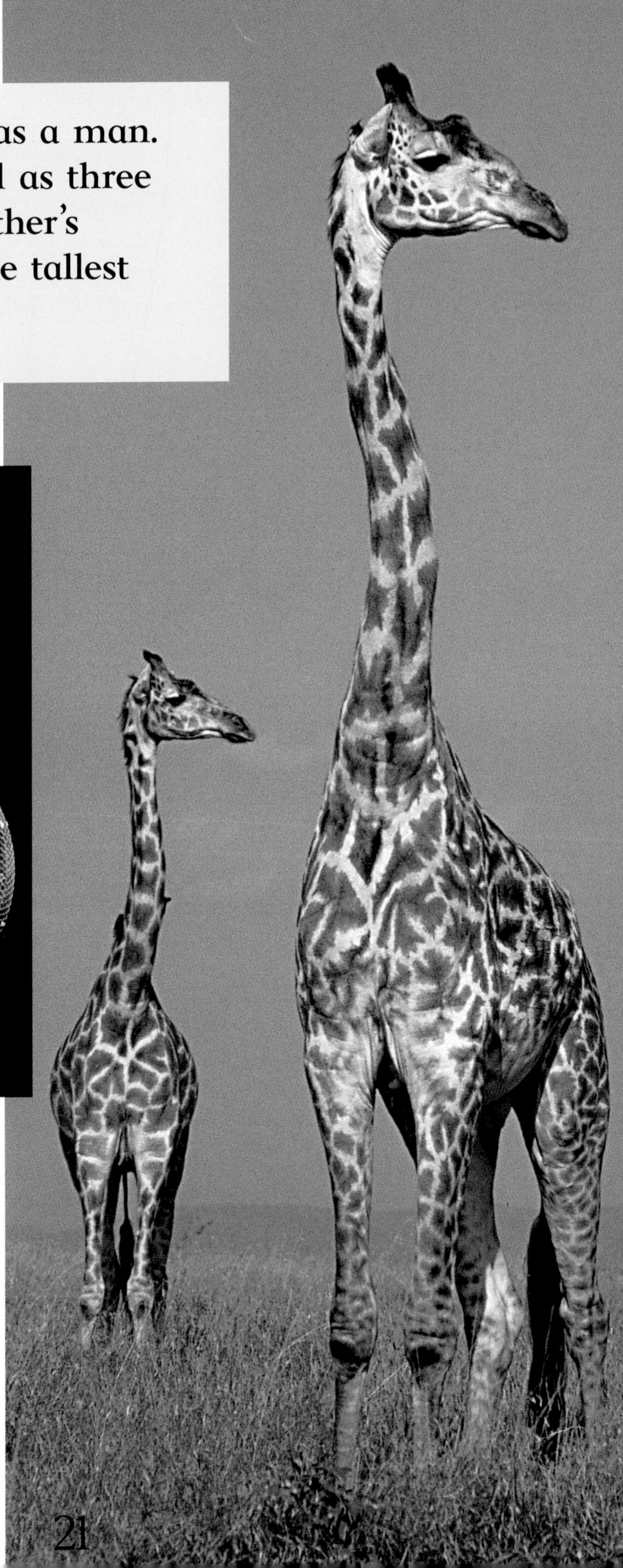

Do we get heavier as we grow?

Yes. Everyone gets heavier as they grow from a child into an adult.

Some people are heavy and some people are light. It doesn't matter how big or small we are. The important thing is keeping healthy.

Weigh yourself on some weighing scales. What is your weight in kilograms? Do you weigh more before you go to bed or when you get up? Why do you think this is?

An ostrich egg weighs about 1 kilogram. An adult ostrich weighs more than 150 kilograms - twice as much as a man! The ostrich is the biggest bird in the world.

Some pygmy shrews weigh less than a 5 pence coin, even when they are fully grown! Pygmy shrews are the smallest mammals in the world.

How do we change as we grow?

As well as getting bigger and stronger, we mature as we grow.

Ask your parents for photographs of you as a baby, as a toddler and of you now. Put the pictures in order. How have you changed? How do you think you will change as you grow up?

Maturing means changing from a child into an adult. Your body changes, so you can have children of your own, if you choose.

A tiny caterpillar hatches from an egg. It eats all the time to help it to grow. Then it changes, first into a chrysalis, then into a beautiful butterfly. Adult butterflies mate, and the females lay eggs of their own.

New swans are called cygnets. In just a year they mature from 'ugly ducklings' into beautiful adults. When a swan is three years old, it is ready to have cygnets of its own.

How can I help myself grow?

You can help yourself grow by eating the right foods. Exercise and rest are important, too.

As you grow, your body needs food to build your bones and muscles. Food gives you energy and the right food also helps you to stay healthy.

Regular exercise and sports such as football, martial arts and blading help your heart and muscles grow strong. You should try to exercise every day.

Sleep is important, too. You must rest your body to give it time to make repairs and grow.

Glossary

hatch
When a baby animal breaks out of its egg.

knowledge
The things we know.

mammal
An animal with hair that feeds on its mother's milk as a baby.

mate
When a male and a female (father and mother) pair to make babies.

moult
When an animal loses its old shell, skin, fur or feathers to grow a new outside layer.

parent
A mother or father.

pouch
A body part that looks like a pocket or bag. A female kangaroo keeps her baby in a pouch on her stomach.

weighing scales
We stand on weighing scales to find out how heavy we are.

Index

Animal index and quiz

Use your animal index to find the answers to this animal quiz!

- Where do crocodile babies grow?
- How heavy is an adult ostrich?
- How does a spider learn how to spin a web?
- How do penguins look after their babies?
- How much taller is a giraffe than a man?
- How does a caterpillar change into a butterfly?